AWESOME VALUES IN FAMOUS LIVES

Dave Thomas

Honesty Pays

Barbara Kramer

Enslow Elementary

an imprint of

Enslow Publishers, Inc.

40 Industrial Road

Enslow Elementary, an imprint of Enslow Publishers, Inc.

Enslow Elementary® is a registered trademark of Enslow Publishers, Inc.

Library of Congress Cataloging-in-Publication Data

Kramer, Barbara.
   Dave Thomas : honesty pays / Barbara Kramer.—1st ed.
      p. cm. — (Awesome values in famous lives)
   Includes bibliographical references and index.
   ISBN 0-7660-2375-3 (hardcover)
   1. Thomas, R. David, 1932–2002—juvenile literature. 2. Wendy's International.
3. Restaurateurs—United States—Biography. I. Title. II. Series.
TX910.5.T56K73 2004
338.7'6167495'092—dc22

                                        2004004503

Printed in the United States of America

10 9 8 7 6 5 4 3 2 1

To Our Readers: We have done our best to make sure all Internet Addresses in this book were active and appropriate when we went to press. However, the author and the publisher have no control over and assume no liability for the material available on those Internet sites or on other Web sites they may link to. Any comments or suggestions can be sent by e-mail to comments@enslow.com or to the address on the back cover.

Every effort has been made to locate all copyright holders of material used in this book. If any errors or omissions have occurred, corrections will be made in future editions of this book.

Contents

CHAPTER 1

An Early Dream

Lights! Camera! Action! A film crew was at the racetrack making a television commercial for Wendy's restaurants. Dave Thomas, founder of Wendy's, grinned with excitement. A famous racecar driver named Darrell Waltrip was letting Dave drive his car.

In the commercial, Darrell played a joke on Dave. While Dave zoomed around the racetrack,

Darrell was secretly eating Dave's lunch, a great big hamburger from Wendy's.

People liked the Wendy's ads because Dave seemed like a regular guy. They saw him as honest, someone they could trust. It was not an act. Dave often called honesty the "number-one ingredient for success." It was something he learned through his own experiences.

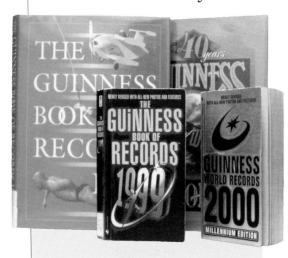

Dave starred in so many Wendy's ads—more than six hundred—that he earned a spot in the Guinness Book of Records.

Dave was born on July 2, 1932, in Atlantic City, New Jersey. He never knew his birth mother. He was adopted by Rex and Auleva Thomas of Kalamazoo, Michigan, when he was about six weeks old. Dave was their only child.

Auleva Thomas died when Dave was five years old, and his father remarried. When that marriage ended in divorce, Dave and his father were on their own once again.

They moved often, traveling all over the Midwest and stopping whenever Rex Thomas could find construction work. Dave and his dad lived in rented rooms in poor areas. "One place had a cement floor and roaches," Dave said later.[2] It was hard to make new friends over and over again. So Dave spent much of his time alone.

The happiest times in Dave's childhood were the summers that he spent with his grandmother Minnie Sinclair. "She taught me early on about

Dave learned about right and wrong from his grandmother.

doing the right thing, working hard, doing a job well and having fun," Dave said.[3]

Sometimes Minnie took Dave along to the restaurant where she worked. Her job was making lunches and washing dishes. Dave liked being in the busy kitchen. He listened to the cook bark out orders. He watched the servers hurry in and out with heaping plates of food.

Dave and his father went to restaurants, too.

They ate out for most of their meals. Dave usually ordered a few hamburgers. "I thought if you didn't have two or three you were starving yourself," he said.[4]

Dave enjoyed those meals because he had his father all to himself.[5] He liked being with his dad, even though they never talked much. The silence gave Dave a chance to watch what was going on around him. He paid attention to details: What was on the menu? Were the employees friendly? How did the restaurant look? Best of all, he liked watching families eating together and having fun.

By the time Dave was eight years old, he knew what he wanted to do when he grew up. "I thought if I owned a restaurant," he said, "I could eat all I wanted for *free*. What could be better than that?"[6]

When Dave was ten, his father married a woman who had two daughters. She was kind to Dave, but he did not feel like part of the family.[7]

Dave got his start in the restaurant business when his family moved to Knoxville, Tennessee. He got a job at a drugstore with a soda fountain. He was twelve years old, but he told the manager that he was sixteen. Dave liked working at the ice cream counter making sundaes and floats. But the job did not last long. The manager fired him when he discovered Dave's real age.

Dave lied again to get a job making sandwiches and serving food at the Regas Restaurant. The two brothers who owned the restaurant did not really believe that Dave was sixteen, but they

The Price of a Burger

When Dave was born, in 1932, a hamburger at a restaurant cost about five cents.

did not fire him because he was such a good worker. Dave had lied about his age, but he soon learned that lies can hurt.

Dave was twelve when he started working at the Regas Restaurant.

CHAPTER 2

Hamburger Cook in Training

Dave was thirteen years old when his grandmother Minnie told him that he was adopted. He was angry that no one had told him sooner. "No one trusted me with the truth," he later said. "I didn't like it at all. It burned me up."[1]

Dave's family moved to Fort Wayne, Indiana, in 1947. Dave was sad to leave the Regas Restaurant,

Fort Wayne is the second biggest city in Indiana.

but he quickly landed a job near his new home. He was hired to clean up dirty tables at the Hobby House Restaurant owned by Phil Clauss.

A few months later, Dave's father told him they were moving again. Dave said no. He had friends at the Hobby House, and he was tired of moving.

He rented a room at the YMCA, and his family left town without him. Dave was fifteen years old and on his own.

Dave worked nights, getting home about one o'clock in the morning. Then, after only a few hours of sleep, it was time for school. Before long, Dave was feeling all worn out. He quit school at the end of tenth grade. He worked at the Hobby House until 1950, when he left to join the army.

Dave reported for military duty at Fort Benning, Georgia. He soon got a chance to attend the army's Cook and Baker's School.

"I thought if I owned a restaurant," said Dave, "I could eat all I wanted for *free*. What could be better than that?"

After the eight-week course, he was promoted to sergeant. "Being a staff sergeant at the age of eighteen was quite an honor, and getting promoted was exciting," Dave said.[2] He was then shipped off to an army base in Frankfurt, Germany.

In Germany, Dave worked as a cook in the dining hall. There, he helped feed about two thousand soldiers a day.

Dave liked his job at the Hobby House Restaurant.

Dave also volunteered to work in the kitchen of the Enlisted Men's Club. After a while, he was hired as the assistant manager of the club.

The club was a great place for soldiers to get together, relax, and have a drink. Not many people ate there, so the club was making only about $40 a day from food sales. Dave believed that the soldiers wanted foods they had enjoyed back home. He changed the menu, adding hot roast beef sandwiches, hamburgers, and chicken in

In the army, Dave cooked food for other soldiers.

a basket. The new items were a big hit. Before long, the club was making about $700 a day in food sales.

Dave stayed in Germany until the end of his three-year term in the army. Then he went back to work at the Hobby House as a cook.

There was a new waitress at the restaurant, named Lorraine Buskirk. She took orders from people in the dining room and gave them to Dave in the kitchen. When food was ready to serve, Dave rang a bell to call the waitresses.

One day, Dave wanted Lorraine to hurry up, so he just kept ringing the bell. Lorraine marched over to Dave carrying two plates of food. "Listen," she said, "would you like me to serve this food or do you want to wear it?"[3]

Dave had met his match. He and Lorraine began meeting after work for a sandwich or a cup of coffee. They became good friends. In 1954, less than a year later, they got married. Their daughter Pam was born the following year.

Phil Clauss opened another restaurant, called the Hobby Ranch House, in 1956. He promoted Dave to assistant manager and put him in charge of the new restaurant.

What Is Success?

Dave believed that happiness equals success. In an essay that he wrote when he was in the tenth grade, Dave said, "If you're happier driving a truck than being president of a bank, drive a truck. You've got to be happy."[4]

Over the next few years, the Thomases had more children. A son, Kenny, was born in 1956. Then came two more daughters, Molly and Melinda. With a larger family to support, Dave was looking for a way to make more money. He soon got that chance.

CHAPTER 3

Young Millionaire

Phil Clauss owned four Kentucky Fried Chicken (KFC) restaurants in Columbus, Ohio. All of them were losing money. Phil asked Dave to help. Could Dave turn them into money-making restaurants? If Dave could do that, Phil would make him part owner.

Dave's friends warned him that he was making a mistake. Even Colonel Harland Sanders, the founder of KFC, told Dave not to do it. Sanders said the restaurants were in bad shape. It would be impossible to fix them. But Dave saw it as a step toward owning his own business, and his wife, Lorraine, agreed. In 1962, Dave Thomas and his family moved to Columbus.

Could Dave save four failing KFC restaurants?

First Dave hired new managers who had more experience in running restaurants. Then he gave each restaurant a fresh coat of paint. Making everything look better "would be good for the employees as well as the customers," he said.[1]

He also advertised more. He did not have money to pay for all the ads, so he made trades. One time, he swapped buckets of fried chicken for radio commercials.

Another daughter, Lori, was born in March 1967. Dave loved his family, but he did not know how to relax and spend time with his children. He had been working since he was twelve years old. "He was always overtired," said one of his daughters. "He really didn't know how to treat kids, didn't know how to go to a baseball game."[2]

By 1967, the four KFC restaurants were making money, and Dave had become a part owner. The next year, Phil and Dave sold the restaurants.

Dave and Lorraine Thomas with Colonel Sanders, left.

Thanks to the chicken business, Dave was a millionaire.

Dave's share of the sale made him a millionaire at the age of thirty-five. He and Lorraine celebrated by having a swimming pool built in their backyard. The pool was shaped like a chicken.

Chicken had made Dave rich, but he still liked a big juicy hamburger best. He began making plans for his own hamburger restaurant.

Dave remembered watching families eating together and having fun. He imagined a place where families could enjoy good food at a good price.

Dave knew that to be successful, his restaurant needed to be different from other hamburger places. Other fast-food restaurants made sandwiches ahead of time and kept them warm under a heat lamp. Dave never liked that. He served all his hamburgers hot off the grill. He used fresh beef instead of frozen patties.

Wendy's sandwiches were made-to-order, and customers could choose up to eight toppings. Dave's favorite was a hamburger with cheese, mustard, pickles, and onions.

Who Is Wendy?

When Dave's daughter Melinda was born, her older brother and sisters had trouble saying her name. So they called her "Wenda." Over time, "Wenda" became "Wendy," and the nickname stuck. Eight-year-old Wendy, with her freckles and red hair, was just the image Dave wanted for his family restaurant.

Wendy's hamburgers were square, and the corners stuck out from the edges of the buns. When people asked Dave why, he told them what his grandmother Minnie always said: "Don't cut corners!"[3] That was her way of teaching him that there were no shortcuts to doing a good job. There was also another reason for the square-shaped hamburgers. They could be laid out side by side on the grill with no wasted space.

Dave opened the first Wendy's Old-Fashioned Hamburgers restaurant in Columbus, Ohio, on November 15, 1969. That day, the line of customers stretched down the block. "He was the hottest thing going," said one of Dave's friends.[4]

Dave's reputation was built on honesty. For Dave, honesty was not only about telling the truth. It also meant treating people right. "One easy thing to do is to be nice to everyone you meet," he said.[5]

In 1970, Dave opened a second Wendy's. It had a drive-through pick-up window so customers could order food from their cars.

Wendy's was the first fast-food place to offer a salad bar and baked potatoes across the nation.

Wendy's was also one of the first fast-food restaurants with a pick-up window.

Dave decided to start a chain of Wendy's restaurants. He imagined that one day, there would be Wendy's restaurants all across the country. Anyone who wanted to own a Wendy's restaurant had to ask Dave first. All of them had to follow Dave's rules. The other Wendy's were called franchise restaurants. The first one opened in 1972.

CHAPTER 4

Wendy's Dad

By 1982, the Wendy's chain had 2,430 franchise stores. Dave decided to take a break from working so hard. He turned the running of the company over to a team of managers.

For the first time in his life, Dave had free time to do whatever he wanted. He and his wife moved to their winter home in Fort Lauderdale, Florida.

Dave played golf and enjoyed his sailboat. When he got tired of sailing, he traded his huge boat for a golf course in Columbia, South Carolina. He also invested in other companies, including a car dealership.

For Dave, honesty also meant treating people right.

At first, Wendy's did well without its founder. In 1985, the company enjoyed its best year ever. Then sales started slipping, and some restaurants closed. Dave said the restaurant owners were getting sloppy. They were not paying attention to important details like clean restaurants, quality food, and friendly service.

Dave started traveling around the country to visit Wendy's restaurants. At each one, he first headed behind the counter to meet the workers. He liked

Dave visited a new Wendy's, built on the spot where the Hobby House restaurant used to be.

to introduce himself as Wendy's dad. He talked to the franchise owners about how they could make improvements.

Dave never grew tired of talking about hamburgers. One day, one of the people at the company's ad agency had an idea: Why not put Dave in his own television commercials? After all, nobody knew more about Wendy's than Dave.

When Dave dropped in on his franchise restaurants, he often stopped to flip a few burgers on the grill.

The first commercials ran in 1989. Dave had never done any acting, and he seemed a bit stiff. Then the company told Dave to relax and just be himself. These new TV ads were a big hit because they were funny. In one ad, Dave was seated in a fancy restaurant. As he eyed the small food serving, he wished he were at Wendy's, enjoying a big juicy hamburger.

The Wendy's television ads made Dave famous, but he never forgot his simple past. "I'm just a hamburger cook," he often said.[1]

Dave used his riches to help others. Over the years, he had

"Where's the Beef?"

The earlier Wendy's television spots were funny, too. A 1984 ad campaign featured a wrinkled, gray-haired actress, Clara Peller. Clara ordered a burger at a fast-food restaurant—not Wendy's—and a huge bun with a tiny hamburger was placed in front of her. "Where's the beef?" she demanded in a loud voice.

The ads were a huge success. People all over the country picked up the saying. "Where's the Beef?" they demanded whenever they expected to get more for their money.

given money to many charities, especially those for children. He donated large amounts to children's hospitals and to camps for children with physical and emotional problems. He was involved with the Children's Home Society of Florida, which helped abused and homeless children. He gave money to many colleges and universities.

Now Dave wanted to do even more. He decided to speak out and use his own life as an example to help others.

Dave's Bloopers

The Wendy's ads starring Dave were a big success, but filming them was never easy. Dave had a habit of mixing up words. He made mistakes and bumped into furniture.

Dave refused to quit until an ad was just right. One day, after doing one scene about sixty times, somebody from the advertising agency kidded Dave. "Remember we just told you to be yourself?" he asked. "Well . . . why don't you try being someone else?"[2]

People liked the Wendy's ads because Dave
was just a regular guy—friendly and funny.

Dave said, "If just one child is adopted,
all our efforts will be worth it."[3]

CHAPTER 5

"Most Likely to Succeed"

For many years, Dave rarely talked about being adopted. He did not lie about it; he just never said anything. After a while, he decided he was not being honest. "Honesty doesn't mean hiding in the weeds; it means stepping out and telling the truth," he said.[1] He decided to talk about adoption.

Dave believed that every child deserves a loving home.

DAVE THOMAS FOUNDATION FOR ADOPTION

Once Dave started talking, things began to happen. In 1990, President George H. W. Bush asked Dave to be national spokesperson for a program called Adoption Works . . . For Everyone.

Dave talked to many companies about adoption. For Wendy's workers, he set up a program to pay for some of the expenses of adopting a child. Dave went to the U.S. Congress to ask for laws to make adoption easier and less expensive for parents.

In 1991, Dave published a book about his life, *Dave's Way: A New Approach to Old-Fashioned Success.* Profits from the sales of his book went to the Dave Thomas Foundation for Adoption, which he founded in 1992.

Dave was always honest and open, even about his mistakes. He told students to work hard in school and get a good education. He said that quitting school was the biggest mistake of his life. "Who knows what more I could have achieved if I'd stayed in school and went to college?" he said.[2]

Dave had always felt bad about quitting school.[3] In 1993,

Golf tournaments at Dave's golf course raised money for charity.

forty-five years after he dropped out, he decided to do something about it. He studied with a tutor for three months. Then he took a seven-hour test to earn a special high school diploma called a GED (General Equivalency Diploma).

Dave was sixty years old when he got his diploma. Students at Coconut Creek High School in Fort Lauderdale, Florida, made him an honorary member of their graduating class. They invited Dave and Lorraine to their senior prom and voted Dave "Most Likely to Succeed."[4]

In 1994, Dave's second book, *Well Done! The Common Guy's Guide to Everyday Success*, was published. Dave wrote about the qualities that help a person become successful. Honesty was at the top of his list.

Two years later, Dave suffered a heart attack and had heart surgery. After he recovered, he was careful to watch his weight and get more exercise.

Dave was so proud when he finally earned a diploma.

Dave and his wife, Lorraine, broke ground for
the Children's Home Society in Florida.

Dave stayed active with his work for adoption and his role as the spokesman for Wendy's restaurants. When he began to have more health problems, his doctors said he had to slow down. Dave cut back on his television appearances, doing only small parts of the Wendy's ads instead of the whole commercials.

Dave died on January 8, 2002, after a long battle with liver cancer. He was sixty-nine years old. Wendy's had lost not only its founder, but also its heart. Even people who had never met Dave felt that they had lost a friend. They knew him from the television ads.

Wendy's customers honored Dave by ordering their hamburgers the way he liked them: with cheese, mustard, pickles, and onions.

"Do the right thing," Dave often said, and he followed his own advice.[5] When Dave promised to do something, he did it. He helped others by giving of his time and money. These were the right things to do.

For Dave, they were also the honest things to do. Honesty was a key to Dave's success. It helped him build his business empire and earned him respect from people all over the world.

Timeline

1932   Born in Atlantic City, New Jersey on July 2; adopted by Rex and Auleva Thomas of Kalamazoo, Michigan.

1944   Begins working at the Regas Restaurant.

1950   Enlists in the U.S. Army.

1953   Finishes his service in the army; returns to work at the Hobby House Restaurant in Fort Wayne, Indiana.

1954   Marries Lorraine Buskirk.

1962   Takes over four failing KFC restaurants in Columbus, Ohio.

1968   Sells the KFC restaurants and becomes a millionaire.

1969   Opens his first Wendy's Old-Fashioned Hamburgers restaurant on November 15.

1990   Becomes national spokesperson for Adoption Works . . . For Everyone; sets up an adoption program for Wendy's workers.

1992   Starts the Dave Thomas Foundation for Adoption.

1993   Earns his General Equivalency Diploma (GED).

2002   Dies on January 8.

Words to Know

charity—A group of people or a fund of money that helps needy people.

franchise—A business that is part of a chain of stores that have the same name and sell the same products.

General Equivalency Diploma (GED)—A paper that can be used instead of a high school diploma. A GED is earned by passing a written test.

honorary—Given as an honor.

invest—Using money to buy something, such as a business, with the belief that it will make more money.

reputation—What people think about someone.

tutor—A teacher who works with one student at a time.

Chapter Notes

CHAPTER 1.
An Early Dream

1. Dave Thomas with Ron Beyma, *Well Done! The Common Guy's Guide to Everyday Success* (Grand Rapids, Mich.: Zondervan Publishing House, 1994), p. 27.

2. Carrie Shook, "Dave's Way: Any Affluent Person Can Write Checks for Charity, But How Many Are Willing—As Dave Thomas Is—To Give Freely of Their Time?" *Forbes*, March 9, 1998, p. 127.

3. "Dave Thomas: American Businessman Founder of Wendy's Restaurants," *Biography Today*, April 1996, p. 111.

4. Scott Hume, "Dave Thomas," *Restaurants & Institutions*, July 15, 2000, p. 29.

5. R. David Thomas, *Dave's Way: A New Approach to Old-Fashioned Success* (New York: G.P. Putnam's Sons, 1991), p. 28.

6. Marilyn Achiron, "Dave Thomas Putting His Money Where His Heart Is, the Man from Wendy's Crusades for Adoption," *People*, August 2, 1993, p. 86.

7. Thomas, *Dave's Way*, p. 29.

CHAPTER 2.
Hamburger Cook in Training

1. Jane Shealy, "His Own Brand of Success," *Success*, November 2000.

2. R. David Thomas, *Dave's Way: A New Approach to Old-Fashioned Success* (New York: G.P. Putnam's Sons, 1991), p. 57.

3. Thomas, p. 69.

4. Shealy, "His Own Brand of Success."

CHAPTER 3.
Young Millionaire

1. R. David Thomas, *Dave's Way: A New Approach to Old-Fashioned Success* (New York: G.P. Putnam's Sons, 1991), p. 94.

2. Marilyn Achiron, "Dave Thomas Putting His Money Where His Heart Is, the Man from Wendy's Crusades for Adoption," *People*, August 2, 1993, p. 88.

3. Douglas Martin, "Dave Thomas, 69, Wendy's Founder, Dies," *New York Times*, January 9, 2002, p. B9.

Chapter Notes

4. Amy Zuber, "Industry Mourns Wendy's Founder Thomas: Icon Succumbs to Cancer at 69," *Nation's Restaurant News*, January 21, 2002, p. 1.

5. Edmonds Community College, "Dave Thomas," © 2004, <http://future.edcc .edu/_perspectives/Dave_Thomas.php> <http://edcc.edu/future2/persp_dave.stm> (June 14, 2004).

CHAPTER 4.
Wendy's Dad

1. Barbara Lippert, "The Natural: Dave Thomas Couldn't Act, But He Connected with Viewers Brilliantly," *Adweek Eastern Edition*, January 14, 2002. p. 16.

2. Wendy's International Inc., © 2003, "Dave Thomas Biography" <http://www .wendys.com/dave/flash.html> (August 19, 2004).

3. Oldemark LLC, © 2000, "News: Press Release, May 7, 2002," <http://www .davethomasfoundationforadoption.org> (August 19, 2004).

CHAPTER 5.
"Most Likely to Succeed"

1. Dave Thomas with Ron Beyma, *Well Done! The Common Guy's Guide to Everyday Success* (Grand Rapids, Mich.: Zondervan Publishing House, 1994), p. 27.

2. Wendy's International Inc., © 2003, "Dave Thomas Biography" <http://www .wendys.com/dave/flash.html> (June 14, 2004).

3. Carmen J. Lee, "Wendy's Owner Has Meaty Message," *Pittsburgh Post-Gazette*, April 1, 1993, p. B4.

4. Marilyn Achiron, "Dave Thomas: Putting His Money Where His Heart Is, The Man from Wendy's Crusades for Adoption," *People*, August 2, 1993, p. 88.

5. Amy Zuber, "Industry Mourns Wendy's Founder Thomas: Icon Succumbs to Cancer at 69," *Nation's Restaurant News*, January 21, 2002, p. 1.

Learn More

"Dave Thomas: American Businessman, Founder of Wendy's Restaurants," *Biography Today*, April 1996, pp. 110–116.

Helmer, Diana Star. *Let's Talk About Adoption*. New York: PowerKids Press, 1999.

Peacock, Nancy. *Dave Thomas*. Philadelphia: Chelsea House Publishers, 2000.

Powell, Jillian. *Adoption*. Austin, TX: Raintree Steck-Vaughn, 2000.

Schaefer, Lola M. *Fast Food Restaurant (Who Works Here)*. Chicago: Heinemann Library, 2001.

Dave Thomas: *Made to Order*, A & E Home Video, 2000.

Internet Addresses

Wendy's corporate website features a tribute to Dave Thomas. It includes a short biography, quotes, and many photos.

<http://www.wendys.com/dave/flash.html>

Read more about Dave and adoption. Click on "News" for some adoption success stories.

<http://davethomasfoundationforadoption.org/html/resource/dave.asp>

Index

Pages with photographs are in **boldface** type.